From the Air

First published in Great Britain in 2010 by
The Derby Books Publishing Company Limited
3 The Parker Centre,
Derby, DE21 4SZ.

A catalogue record for this book is available
from the British Library.

ISBN 978-1-85983-779-5

Printed and bound by Progress Press, Malta.

Cattle grazing in a lush
Keynsham field.

David Goddard

Bristol

From the Air

DB PUBLISHING

Bristol Planetarium in Millennium Square, part of Explore–At–Bristol, located in Harbourside.

CONTENTS

ACKNOWLEDGEMENTS

A personal thank you to my ever-patient wife Maxine and my two gorgeous children Jack and Faith.

I would like to thank the following people of Bristol for their suggestions on sites to film in and around the city: Councillor Chris Willmore, Yate Town Council; Kerry McCarthy, Labour MP for Bristol East; Angeline Barrett; Peter Gould; Ken Taylor; Julian Lea-Jones; Mike Leigh; Laurinda Brown; Maggie Shapland; and Mike Manson.

A very big thank you to the hundreds of people around Bristol who volunteered suggestions, some of whom had very emotional connections to the buildings and villages photographed.

Also to Lloyd Taylor for his outstanding flying; Mel Cubbley, Skytax Aviation; Michael Denham for his helicopter services; Daphne Kurzberg for her proofreading skills; Ian Kraweckyj, technical support.

And my mother, Mary Goddard Linehen.

David Goddard, 2010

INTRODUCTION

This book is an aerial journey around the city of Bristol and its glorious countryside, exploring its architecture, industrial achievements and heritage, while searching for some of its lost landmarks.

On the first day of this project I found myself flying east up the Bristol Channel at 400ft, wondering where this city of half a million people was.

I turned right before the Severn bridges, amid the Avonmouth Docks, and followed the River Avon. Car storage areas gave way to housing estates, and golf courses faded into the ruined Dock at Sea Mills. Bronze-coloured cliffs rose up out of the river to form an imposing gorge. Suddenly I was faced with a beautiful manmade structure spanning the 702ft chasm, the Clifton Suspension Bridge. After a protracted gaze my eyes were drawn to the immense limestone conurbation appearing behind Clifton: the city of Bristol.

A tapestry of mediaeval, Georgian and cutting-edge architecture; church spires breaking the rooflines in all directions; fresh water meandering around the city on three sides, bridges far and wide. Even from this height it is very apparent that Bristol is an area of extremes and contrasts, from the 700-year-old Gothic cathedral in College Green and the Merchant Taylor's Almshouses of 1701 to the 1970s Roman Catholic cathedral in Clifton Downs and the Mall shopping centre in Broadmead. This contrast widens when flying east on the southern edge of Bristol, with the housing of Withywood on my left and on my right the outstanding natural beauty of the Chew Valley.

Above the old docks you can trace the engineering legacy of Isambard Kingdom Brunel on the city: the Great Western Railway appearing from Broom Hill, the original long thin structure of Temple Meads Railway Station, the regal SS *Great Britain* and, of course, his landmark Clifton Suspension Bridge.

Old industrial giants are seen all over the city, giving clues to its dominant trading past: the monolithic warehouses surrounding the Floating Harbour, the Old Soap Factory on Straight Street and the electric cargo cranes on Prince's Wharf.

New landmarks have sprung up all over Bristol and the surrounding area, showing the industrial wind of change, such as the Avonmouth and Royal Portbury Docks outside the city, Filton and Bristol International Airport, the immense redevelopment of the old docks and the two nuclear power stations to the north and south-west of the city.

Bristol has a huge cultural vibrancy that is seen from above the city, from the street art of Banksy and the glowing Picton Street Studios to the landmark Art Galleries on Queens Road, its floating music venues and the sheer colour of some of its residential streets, which break away from their limestone neighbours.

I saw many forgotten and lost landmarks from my vantage point, like St Anne's Well, Clifton Top Railway, the Old City Gaol and the foundations of the original Temple Church, built by Knights Templar.

The countryside around Bristol boasts some of the most beautiful and historical landscapes in the UK, from the Mendip Hills in the south to the battle-stained hills of the southern Cotswolds in the north, and from the natural and the manmade splendor of the Chew Valley to the wide expanse and coastline of the Severn Estuary.

These natural escarpments hide the hilltop fort of Hinton, the stately homes of Tyntesfield and Dyrham Park, the cozy hamlets of Blagdon and Chew Stoke, and the mysterious follies of Blaise Castle.

Before starting this project I contacted people who worked, visited and lived in Bristol for their suggestions for places to include in this book. Their ideas have opened my eyes to the allure of this area. I leave this project believing Bristol is an extraordinary place, with striking individuality, a unique industrial and cultural heritage and blessed with jaw-dropping countryside. I look forward to returning.

The City Centre

An aerial view of the city of Bristol.

Brandon Hill, Bristol's oldest park, was given to the city council in 1174. The park hill rises 260ft above the harbour. A small section of the hill is a nature park and was the first of its kind to be established in Britain. Brandon Hill is one of the best-loved parks in Bristol.

Cabot Tower was built on Brandon Hill park to commemorate the achievements of John Cabot. This Tudor Gothic Revival tower is 105ft high and was built in 1898 by W.V. Gough. It overlooks the surrounding area of Clifton, Hotwells, the Floating Harbour and the city centre.

Bristol's premier museum and art gallery on Queens Road was built between 1899 and 1904 by Sir F. Wills in an Edwardian Baroque style. The museum includes sections on natural history, local, national and international archaeology and local industry. The art gallery contains works from all periods, including many international and famous artists, as well as a collection of modern paintings of Bristol. It is run by the city council and has no entrance fee. The City Museum and Art Gallery is one of Bristol's main landmarks.

The old City Museum and Library on Queens Road was built in a Venetian Gothic Revival style in 1867–71 by Foster and Ponton. Once the Bristol University's Old Refectory building, today it is a Brown's Restaurant.

Colston's Almshouses on St Michael's Hill were founded by the noted Bristol philanthropist merchant Edward Colston. They were built in 1691 and then restored in 1861 and again in 1988, and have been designated by English Heritage as a Grade I listed building.

Foster's Almshouses and the Chapel of the Three Kings of Cologne on Colston Street, Bristol. The chapel was originally built in 1504 and then restored in 1861 and 1865. The Almshouses date back to the 1480s, when they were built on bequest of John Foster, the mediaeval Bristol merchant. The building was greatly extended between 1861 and 1883. Today the Almshouses are privately owned.

Canon's Marsh and the Floating Harbour.

SS *Great Britain*, the world's first purpose-built integrated iron steamship. Launched in Bristol in 1843, it was the ambitious creation of Isambard Kingdom Brunel. After 40 years of service and travelling 32 times around the world, the SS *Great Britain* was abandoned in the Falkland Islands. Following an ambitious salvage project in 1970 the ship was returned to the Great Western Dockyard where it was originally built.

The electric cargo cranes on Prince's Wharf, outside the old Bristol Industrial Museum. Built and erected in 1951 by Stothert & Pitt.

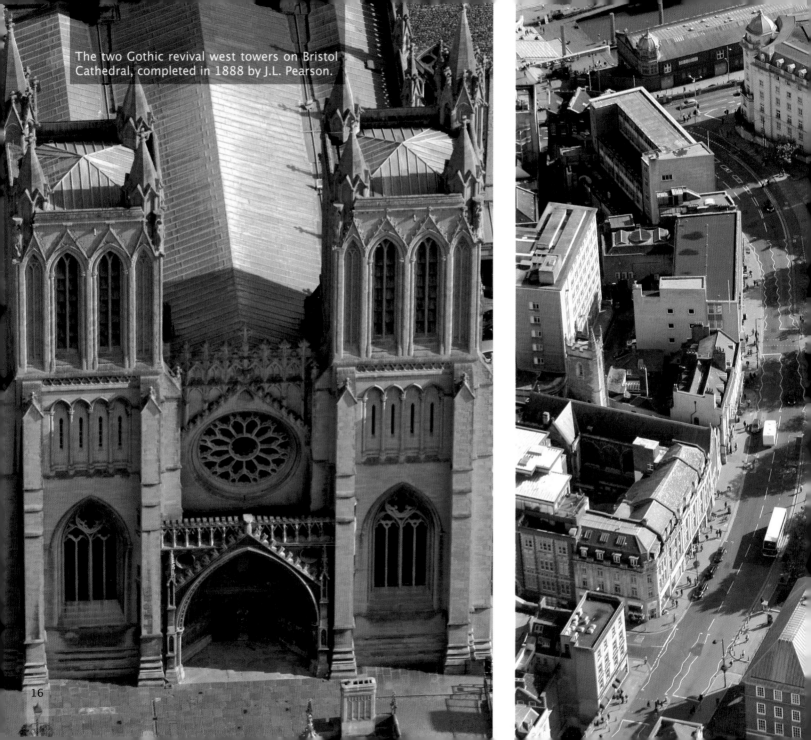

The two Gothic revival west towers on Bristol Cathedral, completed in 1888 by J.L. Pearson.

College Green is an open triangular public space in the centre of Bristol. The original green dates back to the 12th century, when it was a part of the Manor of Billeswick, owned by Robert Fitzharding. The present configuration of the green was created in the early 1950s with the construction of the Council building . On the south side of the Green is the Bristol Central Library, Abbey Gatehouse and Bristol Cathedral. On the western side is The Council House building. To the north-east is St Mark's Church and a collection of banks, retail outlets and offices. The Green is a very popular meeting place for teenagers and college students.

St James Barton Roundabout to the north of the Broadmead area. The roundabout is also locally known as the Bear Pit.

Queen Square is a popular focal point for park based activities during the Harbour Festival. It was built in the 17th century on the old Town Marsh, used for refuse tipping, weapons training and hanging pirates. The square was designed in 1699 and finished in 1727. The square's history has witnessed the Bristol Riots, German bombing and the arrival of a dual carriageway in the middle of the square. Today the square is fully restored to its former design.

Gardiner's warehouse on Straight Street and New Thomas Street, to the east of the city. The Present structure was built in 1865 by William Bruce Gingell. The building was originally a part of Christopher Thomas and Brothers' soap works.

St George's Chapel in Great George Street. Built between 1821 and 1823 in the Greek Revival style and designed by Robert Smirke for the wealthy parishioners of Brandon Hill, today St George's is a popular concert venue.

Portland Square, a mainly Georgian square laid out in the 18th century as one of Bristol's first suburbs. It is located in the St Paul's area, north-east of the city centre. Many of the buildings in the square are Grade I and Grade II listed.

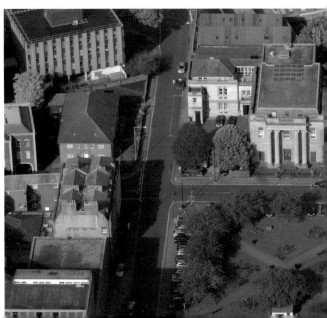

Brunswick Square, to the north-east of the city centre, planned and laid out by the carpenter and surveyor George Tully in 1766.

Wills' Memorial Building, a 215 ft Gothic tower at the top of Park Street. Designed by Sir George Oatley for Sir George A. Wills and Mr Henry Herbert Wills, it was erected in honour of their father, Henry Overton Wills, the first Chancellor of the University. The building was offically opened in 1925 in the presence of George V.

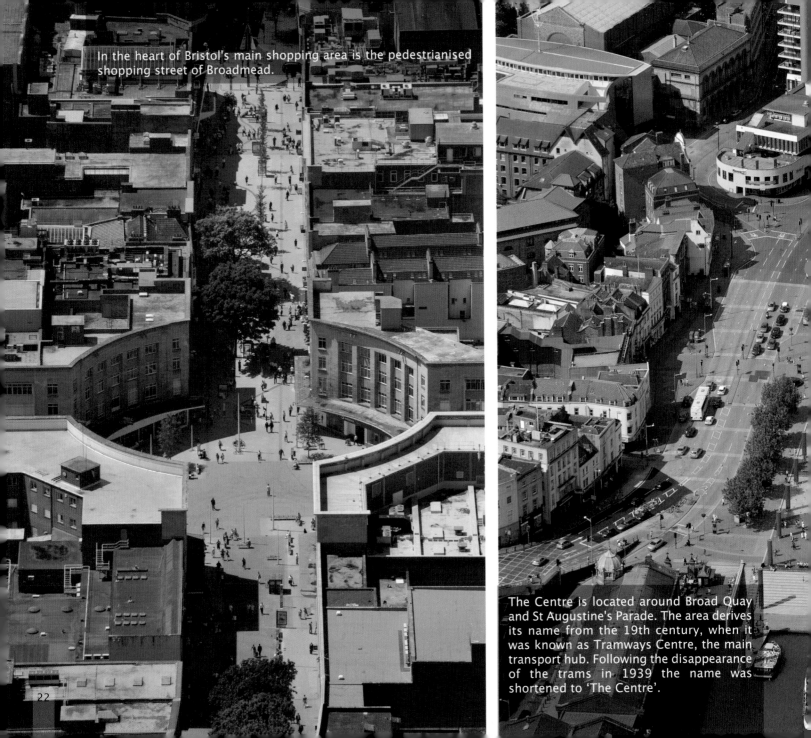

In the heart of Bristol's main shopping area is the pedestrianised shopping street of Broadmead.

The Centre is located around Broad Quay and St Augustine's Parade. The area derives its name from the 19th century, when it was known as Tramways Centre, the main transport hub. Following the disappearance of the trams in 1939 the name was shortened to 'The Centre'.

The Coopers' Hall on King Street, built in 1743–44 by William Halfpenny and rebuilt internally in 1971 when it became the foyer of the Bristol Old Vic. The theatre complex includes the 1766 Theatre Royal, which claims to be the oldest continually operating theatre in England.

Terraced housing on Great George Street, Bristol.

The tiered tower of St Paul's Church, Portland Square, which is situated in the St Paul's area of Bristol.

The varied architectural styles of Bristol are reflected by Bristol Grammar School and the University.

Goldney Student Halls in
Clifton, part of the
University of Bristol.

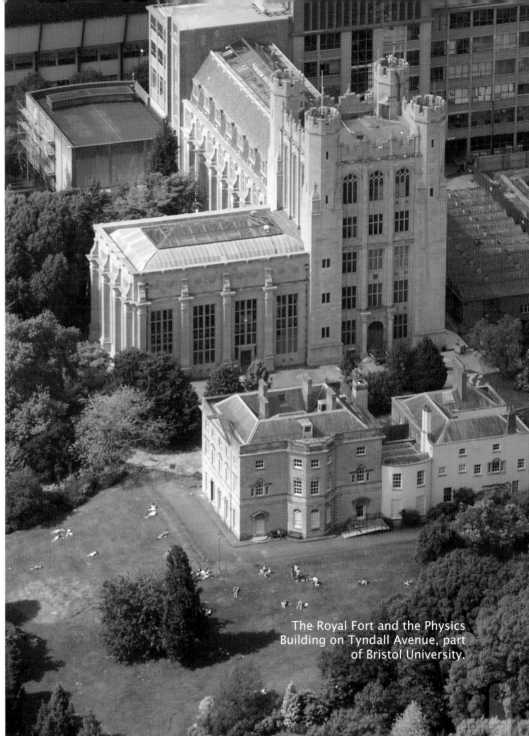

The Royal Fort and the Physics Building on Tyndall Avenue, part of Bristol University.

The Old City

A north-eastern view of the Old City. This is the historic heart of Bristol, and the layout dates back to Saxon times.

Clare Street and Corn Street in the Old City.

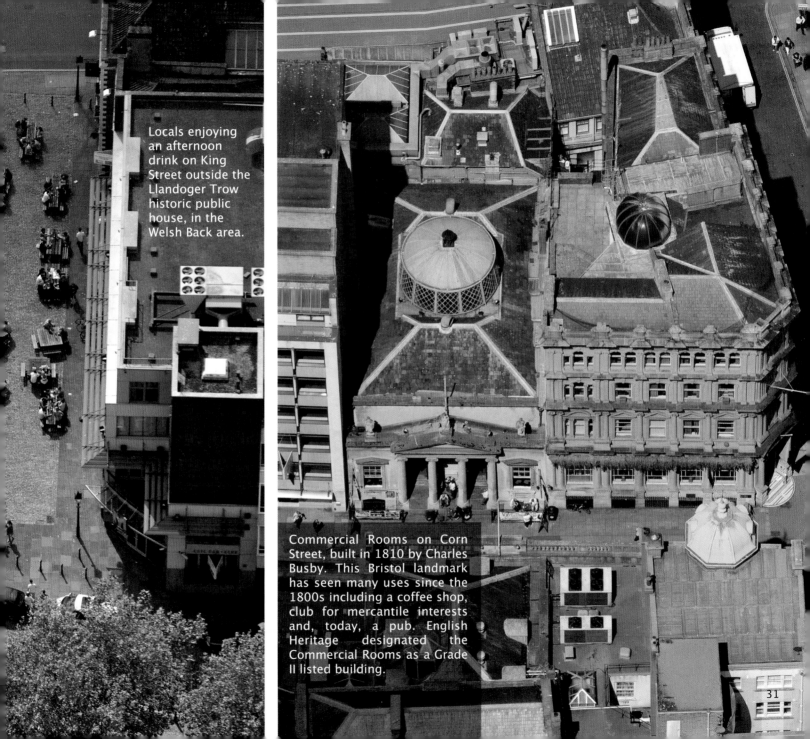

Locals enjoying an afternoon drink on King Street outside the Llandoger Trow historic public house, in the Welsh Back area.

Commercial Rooms on Corn Street, built in 1810 by Charles Busby. This Bristol landmark has seen many uses since the 1800s including a coffee shop, club for mercantile interests and, today, a pub. English Heritage designated the Commercial Rooms as a Grade II listed building.

Locals and tourists enjoying an afternoon drink on Welsh Back near the Llandoger Trow historic public house.

The Church of All Saints on Corn Street, built in the early 12th century. It was altered and enlarged over successive centuries, most notably in 1716 with the addition of the north–east tower by William Paul. It was completed by George Townesend.

Merchant Venturers Almshouses on King Street in Old City were built in around 1696 by the Society of Merchant Venturers for the recuperation of old sailors. Today the Society of Merchant Venturers Almshouses Charity still provides sheltered accommodation.

St Stephen's Church in Stephen's Avenue is the parish church for Bristol. It was built in the 14th century and then rebuilt around 1470.

The Llandoger Trow, a historic public house on King Street. It dates back to 1664 and is one of the last surviving timber-built buildings in Bristol. Many of its original features have been meticulously restored. The building has many myths associated with it involving pirates and smugglers' tunnels. It is hard to define where truth stops and local legends begin.

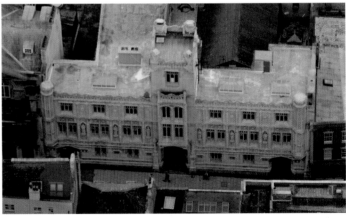

The Guildhall in Broad Street, Old City, was built in 1843–46 in the Tudor Gothic Revival style by R.S. Pope.

The old Scottish Provident Building on Clare Street was built in 1903 by Oatley and Lawrence in an Edwardian Baroque style.

This is a view of the historic heart of the city from 1000ft, showing Corn Street, Broad Street, St Nicolas Street and Small Street in the Old City.

The lanes and roads surrounding Bristol's largest and oldest market, St Nicholas' Market in the Old City. The market has the largest collection of independent retailers in Bristol. The entrance is located on Corn Street.

The Channel & Severn Estuary

A view of the Severn Bridge and Second Severn Crossing illustrating the three miles of the River Severn that lies between the two bridges.

A marine dredger in the South Dock at Avonmouth.

The Avonmouth Docks, part of the Port of Bristol, are located on the River Severn, north of the mouth of the River Avon. Avonmouth was opened in 1877 following the purchase of the old dock by the Bristol Corporation in 1884. Today it is one of the UK's major ports.

Grab unloader crane in the Royal Portbury Dock.

Gantry grab crane unloading coal at Avonmouth.

The Royal Portbury Dock, part of the Port of Bristol on the River Severn and south of the Avonmouth Docks. This deepwater dock was built between 1972-1977 and is a major port for the importation and exportation of cars. The site also offers vast storage compounds for cars and in 2003 the Bristol Aviation Fuel Terminal was opened.

Clevedon in North Somerset, 11 miles to the south-west of Bristol. A Victorian seaside town on the Severn Estuary, the resort dates back to the 11th century. Clevedon is built around seven hills, which offer magnificent views across the Severn Estuary and the Somerset countryside. Today Clevedon is a dormitory town for Bristol.

Clevedon Pier opened in March 1869. It was built by the engineers John William Grover and Richard Ward and designed by Hans Price. The Pier is 1020 ft long and partially built from Isambard Kingdom Brunel's second-hand railway tracks. Today Clevedon Pier is the only fully-intact Grade I-listed pier in the country.

To the south of the orignal Severn bridge is the the Second Severn Crossing, spanning 5,128 metres and carrying the M4 motoway into Wales over the Severn Estuary.

Flat Holm gun emplacements from World War Two look out over the Bristol Channel.

Flat Holm in the Bristol Channel and the Welsh city of Cardiff in the background.

Flat Holm Lighthouse stands at 98ft high over the southern tip of the island. There has been a warning light system on the island since the begining of the 18th century, due to its geographical postion in the channel. The present lighthouse was built in 1737.

Flat Holm is an 86-acre island in the Bristol Channel, located 23 miles south-west of Bristol. The island was first inhabited by Anglo-Saxons and Vikings. The island has a wealth of marine and grassland wildlife and has been designated a Nature Reserve and a site of Special Scientific Interest.

Flat Holm jetty.

Oldbury nuclear power station and the River Severn bridges in South Gloucestershire.

On the eastern side of Steep Holm Island below Zig Zag Path is the historic ruin of the island's inn.

The Severn Bridge, a Grade I listed structure, was opened in 1966 by Queen Elizabeth II. The suspension bridge took five years to build at a cost of £8 million. It spans 988m, joining South Gloucestershire to Monmouthshire, Wales.

Knightstone Island, Weston-Super-Mare, Somerset.

North

To the north-east of the city centre is the geometric housing estate surrounding Little Paul Street in Kingsdown.

Western College on Cotham Road was built in 1905–06 by Henry Dare Bryan. It is described as Bristol's best Arts and Crafts building.

High on Star Hill overlooking Stoke Park and the M32 is Dower House. The original house was built here in 1553 by Sir Richard Berkeley. In recent times it became Pur Down Hospital and then Burden Neurological Institute. It closed as a hospital in 1985 and has become a luxury apartment complex.

Blaise Castle House Museum near Henbury. Situated in 400 acres of the Blaise Estate, the house was designed by William Paty and built in 1796–98 for John Harford, a Bristol merchant and banker. The estate was landscaped by Humphry Repton between 1752–1818.

Two MK Airlines aircraft outside one of the large maintenance hangars at Filton Airport. These 747–200s carry cargo all over the world. They have a full–load range of 6,800 nautical miles.

Concorde 216-AF is based at Filton Airport. This Concorde made its final flight home to Filton on 26 November 2003. It has since become a major tourist attraction.

Bristol Filton Airport, or Filton Aerodrome, four miles to the north of the city, opened in 1910. This airport has played a significant role in the history and development of British aviation. It was the birthplace of the Bristol Freighter, Bristol Brabazon, Bristol Fighter, the Britannia and, of course, Concorde. Today the airport is used by general and corporate aviation and also offers extensive aviation maintenance based in the large hangar facilities. Filton is also one of two UK sites that supply engineering and design for Airbus industries.

A landscaped field to the north of Filton Airport, Bristol.

A south-western view of Blaise Castle Estate and Blaise Hamlet in Henbury. In the distance are Lawrence Weston, Avonmouth and the Bristol Channel. Local points of interest in the foreground include the Church of St Mary the Virgin, the Grade II listed Village Hall and the Blaise Castle House Museum.

The castle in the Blaise Estate. The Gothic Castle was built in 1766 by the architect Robert Mylne on Coombe Hill, overlooking Hazel Brook near to the suburb of Henbury.

Henleaze Lake, a former quarry and now an idyllic lagoon on the northern edge of Henleaze. It became the home of the Henleaze Swimming Club in 1919.

Kings Weston House, a Grade I-listed Georgian mansion set in 28 acres of parkland near Kings Weston. The house was designed by Sir John Vanbrugh and built in around 1711 for Edward Southwell. Today the house is a wedding venue and conference centre.

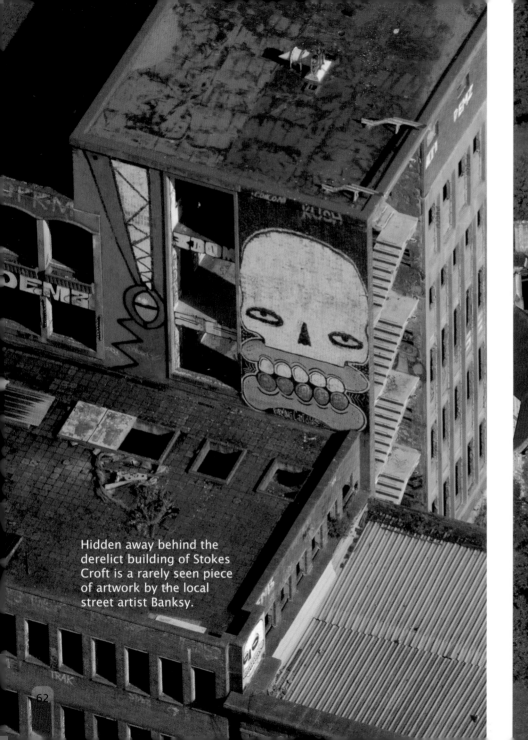

Hidden away behind the derelict building of Stokes Croft is a rarely seen piece of artwork by the local street artist Banksy.

Oatley House and St Monica's Home of Rest, built between 1920–25 by Sir G. Oatley in a Cotswold Elizabethan Revival style for H.H. Wills and Monica Wills. Located on Cotes Lane in Westbury-on-Trym.

South Bristol

A wide-angle view of Ashton Gate,
Bedminster and Southville, to the
south-west of the city.

Temple Church, a historically important ruined church on Victoria Street, also known as Holy Cross Church. Built around 1400 in a Perpendicular Gothic style, the 114-foot tower still leans to the west. The original church on this site was built by the Knights Templar and Robert Earl of Gloucester. It was constructed in a circular stlye in the mid-12th century. The church was bombed in November 1940 during World War Two. Due to the severity of the damage the church was left as a roofless shell. The circular foundations of the original church can be seen in the centre of the existing building.

Dundry village, located on Dundry Hill in the northern part of the Mendip Hills, four miles to the south-west of Bristol. In the centre of the village is the Church of St Michael, the tower built in 1484, the rest built in 1861.

Church of St Mary Redcliffe, on Redcliffe Way, Redcliffe. The original parts of the church date back to the 12th century. The majority of the alterations and enlargements took place in the 15th century. The church's spire reaches a height of 292ft, making it the tallest building in Bristol.

The adventure playground at the Hengrove Leisure Park.

Temple Meads Railway Station. Bristol's main train station, it is celebrated as a great example of Victorian railway architecture.

The main entrance to Temple Meads railway station, originally the Booking Office, built in 1865–78 in a Tudor revival style by Sir Matthew Digby Wyatt for the GWR and the Midland Railway.

This is the limestone façade of the oldest surviving passenger terminus in the world. The Temple Gate entrance to the Old Station was built in 1839–41 by Isambard Kingdom Brunel. Today, it is the British Empire and Commonwealth Museum.

Gaol Ferry footbridge over the River Avon, Southville.

Lime Road, Gathorne Road and Exeter Road in Southville.

The Ashton swing bridge over the River Avon, south-west of Bristol city centre. Opened in 1906 and built by John Lysaght and Co, the original bridge was a double decker, carrying road traffic on the top and two railway lines on the lower deck. The 202ft-long bridge could swing in either direction, allowing access to the river to all vessels at high and mid-tide. The bridge was last swung in 1936.

Hengrove Way and Willmotte.

The huge monolithic warehouses around the Cumberland Basin and River Avon. These buildings, including B Bond Warehouse (top right), were designed and built by William Cowlin and Sons in around 1908.

Whitchurch is a small village over three and a half miles from the city centre, lying on the edge of the Somerset countryside.

Merchants Academy on Gatehouse Avenue. A £30 million state-of-the-art school, it opened on 15 September 2008 in Withywood.

Stevens Cresent, Windsor Terrace, Green Street, William Street and Hill Street in Totterdown.

Kingswood High Street in South Gloucestershire. A large urban area almost four miles to the east of the city of Bristol, in the 18th century Kingswood was a small mining community which echoed to the outdoor preaching of George Whitefield, the Anglican minister who greatly influenced John Wesley in the founding of Methodism.

The River Avon flows around the Conham River Park, which is owned by South Gloucestershire Council. A woodland of maturing broadleaved trees, home to a wide variety of wildlife and fauna with full public access, it is part of the Avon Valley Woodlands near Hanham.

The Lawrence Hill and Easton Road Junction in the area of Lawrence Hill to the east of the city centre.

Siston Court, an Elizabethan manor house, sits in Siston Park, between Pucklechurch and Kingswood, South Gloucestershire. It was built in the 16th century, with further alterations made in the 17th century.

The landscaped grass embankment alongside the A4174 at Mangotsfield, Bristol.

St Anne's Park, a housing estate to the east of the city, surrounded on three sides by the River Avon.

Feeder road bridge between the St Philip's and the St Anne's suburbs of Bristol.

The Traction and Rolling Stock Maintenance Depot in St Philip's Marsh.

The Eye, a new 13-storey residential tower on Temple Quay overlooking the Floating Harbour and Temple Quay Pedestrian Bridge.

The Chimney on Troopers Hill, built in around 1800 for a copper works.

Wick Quarry, situated to the north-east of the village of Wick, is a partly operational limestone quarry.

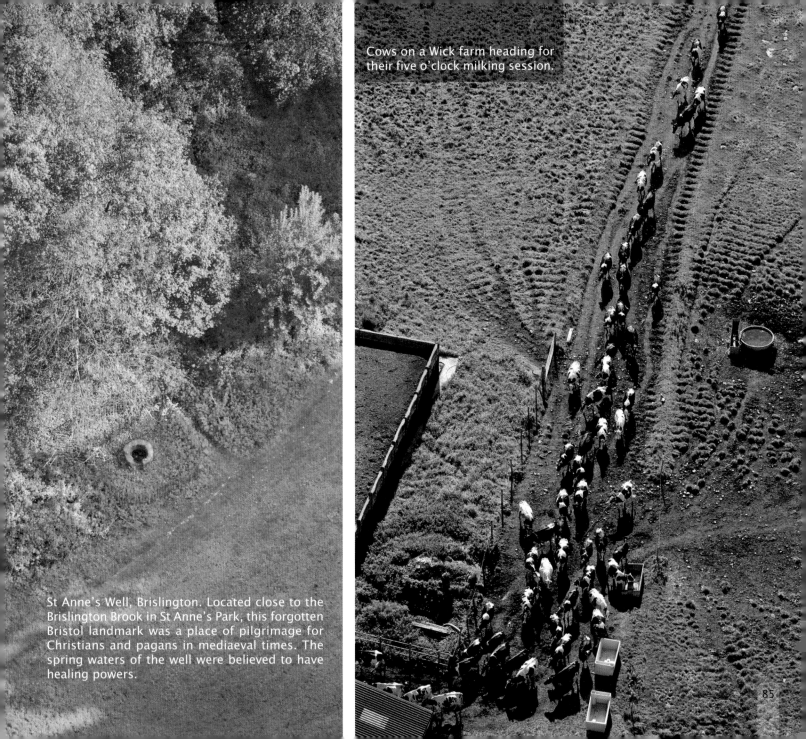

Cows on a Wick farm heading for their five o'clock milking session.

St Anne's Well, Brislington. Located close to the Brislington Brook in St Anne's Park, this forgotten Bristol landmark was a place of pilgrimage for Christians and pagans in mediaeval times. The spring waters of the well were believed to have healing powers.

The contemporary headquarters of a national insurance company at Stoke Gifford in the shadow of Filton Airport.

The Wesleyan Chapel between Blackhorse Road and Waters Road. This Victorian Methodist Chapel was built in 1843. It was last used as a dance school, and today it is derelict waiting for possible redevelopment.

The St Vincent's Works in Silverthorne Lane, built in 1891 for the offices of John Lysaght's Iron Works, is now a Grade II-listed building.

Bristol

Ashton Court Estate comprises 850 acres of woodland and grassland, laid out by Humphrey Repton in the late 18th century. The estate is a very popular recreational area and includes two pitch-and-putt golf courses, horse riding and mountain bike trails, a deer park and a miniature railway. During the summer months the park plays host to many local and international events, including the Bristol International Balloon Fiesta.

89

Ashton Court Railway is situated on the A369 Portishead to Bristol road, and it is operated by the Bristol Society of Model and Experimental Engineers. The Society was founded in 1909 and is one of the oldest in the country. Public Running Days occur on most Sundays from April to October.

The south-western façade of Ashton Court Mansion. In the centre is the core of the original mediaeval building.

Tyntesfield. The original Tyntes Place was a modest building built in 1813 for John Seymour. The house was then transformed into a 25-bedroom Gothic revival palace by William Gibbs in the 1860s. The house is set amid elegant Victorian formal gardens, five miles to the west of Bristol. Tyntesfield was acquired by the National Trust in June 2002.

Leigh Woods on the western bank of the Avon Gorge. This 496 acres of public woodland is a site of Special Scientific Interest, with a wealth of flora and fauna to explore. At the southern end of the forest is Stokeleigh Camp, which dates back to 3BC. In 1909 part of the woodland was donated to the National Trust by George Alfred Wills. In recent years the forest was designated a National Nature Reserve.

Old steamer staging on
Hotwells Road, Hotwells.

The view over the Floating Harbour towards Hotwells, one mile to the south-west of the city centre. Hotwells is named after the hot springs which rise up through the rocks of the local Avon Gorge.

Three miles south–west of the city on Ashton Hill
is the Somerset village of Long Ashton.

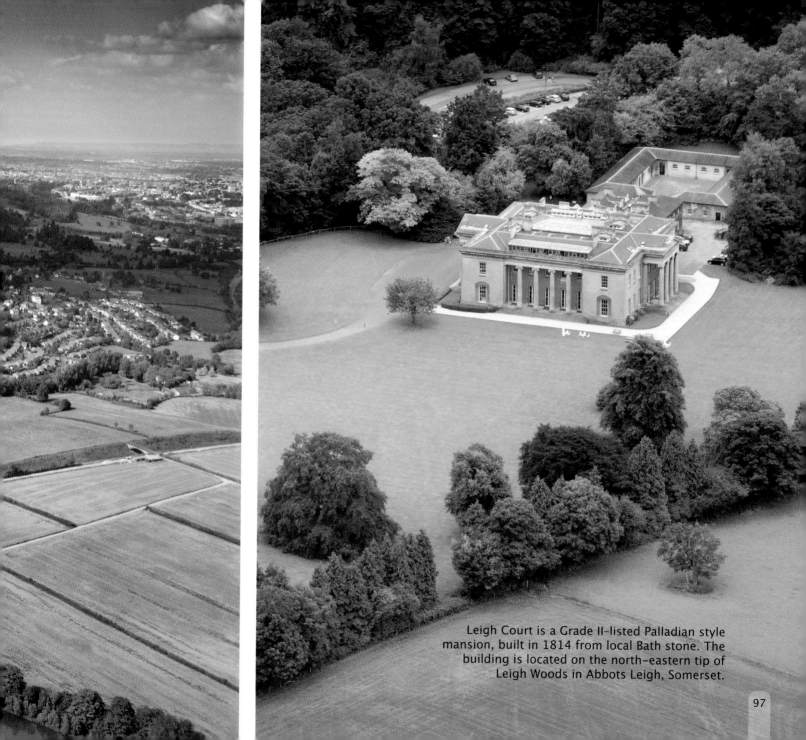

Leigh Court is a Grade II-listed Palladian style mansion, built in 1814 from local Bath stone. The building is located on the north-eastern tip of Leigh Woods in Abbots Leigh, Somerset.

The Countryside

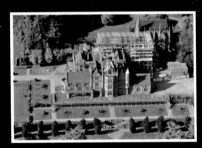

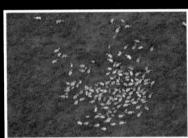

Barrow Gurney, or Barrow Tanks, are three drinking water reservoirs near the village of Barrow Gurney, to the south–west of Bristol. Opened in 1852 by Bristol Water, today these three artificial lakes are also very popular fishing venues.

Barrow Court near Barrow Gurney, North Somerset. Originally a 13th-century Benedictine nunnery, it was converted into a country mansion in 1538 and then rebuilt seven years later. Further alterations took place in 1602 and 1882. Today the house is divided into private residences.

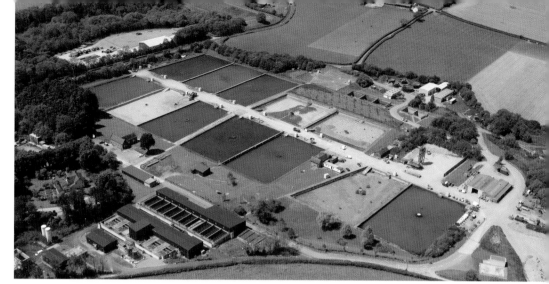

Barrow Gurney treatment works next to the Barrow Gurney Reservoirs. The site was first used by the Bristol Waterworks Company in 1868.

Blagdon Lake is a manmade lake, situated nine miles to the south-east of Bristol, created when the Bristol Waterworks Company dammed the River Yeo in 1891. The reservoir holds 8,456 million litres when full and covers an area of 440 acres. It was originally called the Yeo Reservoir. The pumping station is now a part of the popular visitors' centre which features an original working steam engine and a children's educational facility.

The villages of Blackmoor and Lower Langford are situated 11 miles to the south-west of Bristol, north of the Mendip Hills in Somerset.

Coombe Lodge was built between 1930–35 for Sir George Alfred Wills (president of the Imperial Tobacco Company in Bristol). It is located to the south–west of Blagdon Lake in the Chew Valley. The lodge was designed by Sir George Oatley, an architect who created many landmark buildings in Bristol, including the Royal Infirmary. Today the lodge is used as a beautiful wedding venue and conference centre.

The Bartons cricket ground in Blagdon, overlooked by St Andrew's Church. The ground has been the home of Blagdon and West Mendip Cricket and Quoit Club since 1947.

The village of Blagdon in North Somerset, 10 miles to the south-east of Bristol. The area of Blagdon dates back to AD49, with evidence of a Roman settlement and Roman mines. There have been many major archaeological discoveries to support this. The village is made up of three former settlements: West End, East End and Street End. The village sits in an area of outstanding natural beauty, overlooking Blagdon Lake.

Sutton Court was once a fortified manor near Bishop Sutton. It was built in the early 14th century, with alterations made in around 1450, 1558 and 1700 and a major reconstruction and restoration in 1858–60 by T.H. Wyatt. The building is now a country house, divided into luxury apartments with extensive recreational grounds.

The Iron Age fortification of Hinton Hillfort. It is a short walk to the north of Dyrham Park, believed to be the site of the Battle of Dyrham in AD577.

One of the many old farm ruins found in the Somerset countryside. This one can be found near Pensford.

The River Avon flowing north-east towards Bristol past the Avon Valley Country Park, Keynsham.

The village of Pensford in the Chew Valley, six miles south-east of Bristol in Somerset. Just below the disused North Somerset railway viaduct is the Grade I-listed St Thomas A Beckett Church. In May 1988 Pensford was made a conservation area due to its unique architectural and historic features.

Festivals

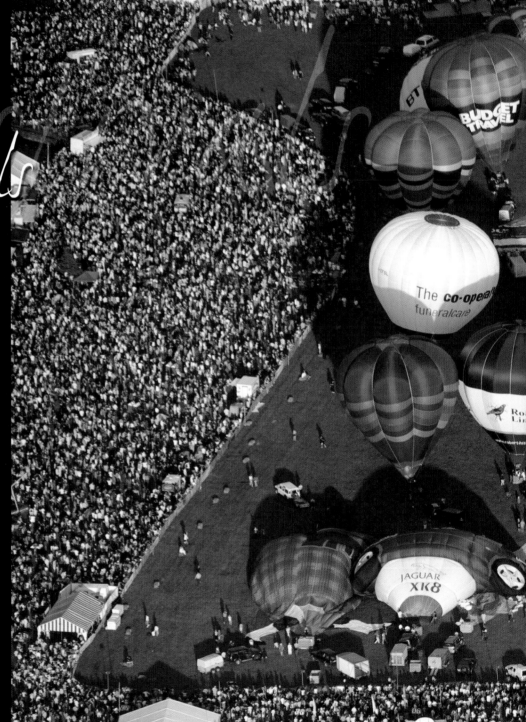

The launch site of the
Bristol International Balloon
Fiesta at Ashton Court.

A western view from 1000ft over Kingswood of the Bristol International Balloon Fiesta. The Fiesta is a mass launch of over 100 balloons from the Ashton Court Estate, one and a half miles to the west of the city. This is one of the largest balloon events in Europe, and many of the balloons taking part are made in Bedminster, Bristol.

Some of the balloons crossing over the River Avon and Ashton Gate.

113

Crowds gather by the observatory on Clifton Down to watch the Bristol International Balloon Fiesta.

A jazz band performs in the Lloyds Amphitheatre, Canon's Marsh, during Bristol Harbour Festival.

Prince Street Swing Bridge, Arnolfini Art Centre and the tall ship *Kaskelot* during the Bristol Harbour Festival.

John Cabot's *Matthew*. This is a replica of the original ship that left Bristol in 1497 and landed on the east coast of Newfoundland and so discovered America. The replica was built in Redcliffe Wharf with green oak frames and Douglas Fir planks, and was completed in two years. Colin Mudie had the task of designing this copy using period illustrations and archaeological data, since no original drawings exist. The new *Matthew* is well established on Bristol's must–see list.

Clifton

Clifton Suspension Bridge has been one of the icon landmarks of Bristol and the south–west of England for almost 150 years. Its majestic design spans the 702ft wide Avon Gorge. The bridge was designed by Isambard Kingdom Brunel in 1829–31 after he won a bridge design competition. Work began in 1836 and stopped in 1840, after the pylons had been completed, due to a lack of money. Work was resumed in 1861 following the death of Brunel. The bridge was completed in 1864 by J. Hawkshaw and W.H. Barlow. The intended Egyptian decoration of the original design was not used.

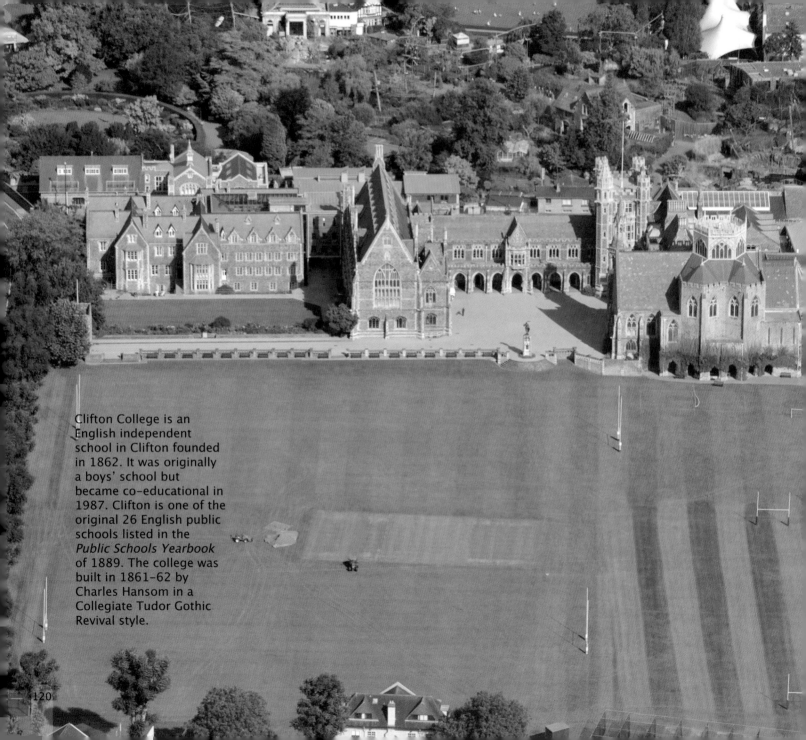

Clifton College is an English independent school in Clifton founded in 1862. It was originally a boys' school but became co-educational in 1987. Clifton is one of the original 26 English public schools listed in the *Public Schools Yearbook* of 1889. The college was built in 1861–62 by Charles Hansom in a Collegiate Tudor Gothic Revival style.

The Victory Arch on College Road, a World War One memorial gatehouse built in 1922 by Charles Holde.

Goldney Hall and the Gothic Tower, built on the site of the previous hall in 1714, possibly by the surveyor George Tully for Thomas Goldney II.

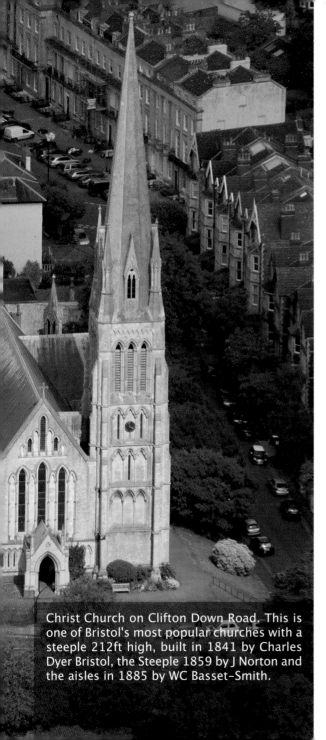

Christ Church on Clifton Down Road. This is one of Bristol's most popular churches with a steeple 212ft high, built in 1841 by Charles Dyer Bristol, the Steeple 1859 by J Norton and the aisles in 1885 by WC Basset-Smith.

The Royal West of England Academy building on Queen's Road in Clifton. Bristol's first official Art Gallery, it was constructed in 1858 and paid for by Bristol Society of Artists, in particular Ellen Sharples. Patrons have included Isambard Kingdom Brunel, the Prince Consort and more recently Queen Elizabeth II.

Queen Elizabeth's Hospital on Jacobs Well Road, built in 1844–47 by Thomas Foster and Son in a Tudor Gothic revival style. Today QEH is an independent school for boys.

An eastern view of Clifton Suspension Bridge, the suburb of Clifton and the city of Bristol from above Leigh Woods.

Another view of the Clifton
Suspension Bridge.

Bristol International Festival of Kites & Air Creations on the Plateau in the Ashton Court Estate. The festival has been a popular attraction in Bristol and the local area since it began in 1986.

Westfield Place, West Mall, Caledonia Place, Princess Victoria Street, Royal York Crescent and the Paragon in Clifton.

The Aquarium.

The Victoria Rooms on Whiteladies Road, Clifton. One of Bristol's landmark buildings, designed by Charles Dyer in the Greek Revival style, it was opened as assembly rooms in 1842 at a cost of £28,000. It became a lively cultural centre, hosting performances from the 19th–century soprano Jenny Lind and readings from Charles Dickens. Today the Victoria Rooms are allocated to the Department of Music, part of Bristol University.

Bristol International Airport at Lulsgate Bottom in North Somerset. The area was first used for aviation when it became a relief landing ground for a Weston-super-Mare Training School in 1940. During World War Two the airfield was used by the RAF, operating Miles Masters, Airspeed Oxfords and Hawker Hurricanes. However, the first plane to land at Lulsgate was a confused German Junkers 88. In the 1950s the airfield was modernised and then reopened in 1957 by Princess Marina, Duchess of Kent. The airport has continued to grow and expand, becoming the ninth busiest airport in the UK.